# THE
# EASY-GOING
# PLANT-BASED
# COOKBOOK

SIMPLE WHOLE-FOOD RECIPES FOR NON-CHEFS,
WITH NO ADDED SUGAR, SALT, OR FAT

by Tom Buschman
photos by Kib Buschman
illustrations by Peg Buschman
editing & design by Karuna Eberl

The Easy-Going Plant-Based Cookbook:
Simple Whole-Food Recipes for Non-Chefs,
With No Added Sugar, Salt, or Fat,

First Edition

by Tom Buschman

Copyright 2020 by Quixotic Books, quixoticbooks.com

ISBN: 978-0-9988589-4-4

Library of Congress Catalog-in Publications Data:
Buschman, Tom
The Easy-Going Plant-Based Cookbook:
Simple Whole-Food Recipes for Non-Chefs,
With No Added Sugar, Salt, or Fat,

Photos by Kib Buschman
Illustrations by Peg Buschman
Editing & design by Karuna Eberl

www.easygoingwfpb.com

Printed in the United States of America by
Versa Press, East Peoria, Illinois

Printed on recycled paper with soy ink and other critical environmental considerations.

I thank my wife, Kib, for dropping whatever she was doing to take photos, whenever I had a new recipe ready. She has been most supportive of my experiments in our new food strategy.
In 2020 we celebrated our 50th wedding anniversary.

This book would only be rough notes if not for the editor and designer, Karuna Eberl. I had a large file with my recipes and thoughts, but it was a total mess and only meant for my use.
If she had not taken an interest in this book, it would have never happened.

*Note: Karuna's writing and other work can be found at wanderingdogcreations.com.*

## LAWYER'S DISCLAIMER

The information contained in this book is based on the experience and research of the author. It is not intended as a substitute for consulting with your physician or other healthcare professionals. The creators, publishers, and distributors of this book are not licensed physicians, medical professionals, or health experts.  Any attempts to diagnose or treat any illness should be done under the direction of a healthcare professional. Full medical clearance should be obtained before beginning or modifying any diet, exercise, or lifestyle program, and physicians should be informed of all nutritional changes. The creators, publishers, and distributors claim no responsibility to any person or entity for any liability, loss, or damage caused, or alleged to be caused, directly or indirectly, as a result of the use, application, or interpretation of the information presented herein.

## TOM'S DISCLAIMER

I poke fun at the Cleveland area, but I think it's the greatest location in the nation. When I started eating whole-foods, plant-based, I was surprised to find that Cleveland has an active whole-foods, plant-based community.

For helpful links and more detail on some of the recipes:
Tom on Instagram: easygoingwfpb
www.easygoingWFPB.com.

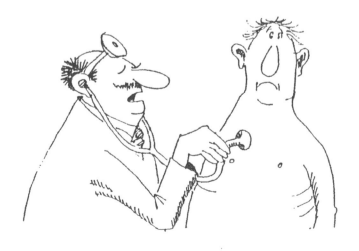

## EDITOR'S NOTE

Tom, the author of this cookbook, is my uncle. His stubborn quest for good health has inspired the eating habits of my branch of the family as well. Thank you, Tom.

Speaking of families, as we were wrapping up this book, Tom's mom Peg, my Grandmama, turned 100 years old. All of the illustrations within were created by her, throughout the years.

Thank you Grandmama, for your creative spirit. We love you.

1992

2018

Grandmama & Karuna (and brother Luke)

# RECILPES

# WHAT'S INSIDE

# ABOUT TOM

I am not a chef. I posses no formal cooking credentials. I'm just a working stiff from Cleveland, Ohio, who switched to a whole-foods, plant-based lifestyle a few years back. To keep it going, I've had to develop recipes that are simple enough to fit into real-life. I wrote this book to share those with my friends and family, who either want to start to eat like this, or who need some help sticking with it.

The benefits of these eating habits are well established and scientifically documented, so I won't rehash that much, except to say that since starting this, my fasting glucose has come down from 99 to 100 to between 87 and 93. My cholesterol has dropped from 280 to 160. My weight is now below what it was in high school. According to my Ormon Body Composition Monitor, my body age is 50. At this writing I am 70. Anorexic I am not. I eat more food more often than ever before.

My overall goal is to maintain healthy cholesterol, glucose, blood pressure, and weight, and to have more energy. My desire is not to live forever but to feel good and be active. I didn't feel bad before, but I can tell the difference. I feel better now.

I'm not telling you what to do. I am not suggesting that my way is the best way. I am only sharing what I am doing. My hope is that you will get some ideas and inspirations from which to develop your own whole-foods, plant-based food strategies. At the very least, I hope you'll get a few laughs.

# TOM'S BEEF WITH VEGAN COOKBOOKS

### JUST BECAUSE IT'S VEGAN, DOESN'T MEAN IT'S HEALTHY

In *The Easy-Going Plant-Based Cookbook*, we mostly avoid:
- added fats, sugars, and salt,
- low-quality carbs, and
- highly-processed crap ingredients.
- We totally avoid meat and dairy.

### TIME-CONSUMING RECIPES ARE IMPRACTICAL FOR EVERYDAY LIFE

We try to keep at bay:
- complicated recipes
- ingredients not found in the local store
- recipes that call for a bit of something that only comes in a big bunch
- recipes that don't keep well, and so are poor for a big batch of leftovers
- recipes that push three mixing bowls, when only one needs to be dirtied
- recipes that require making other recipes from other parts of the book

### PLAY WITH YOUR FOOD

You know what you like more than we do, so:
- experiment
- enjoy the white space for notes, ingredient change-ups, and doodling.

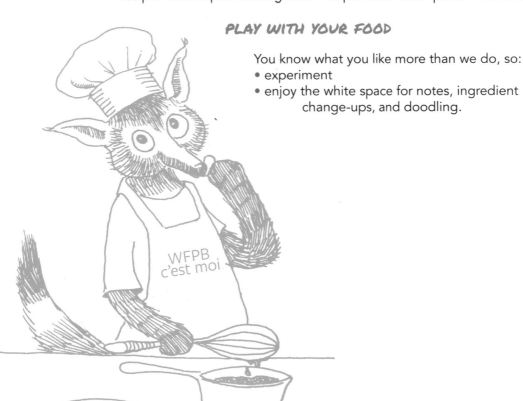

# WHOLE-FOODS, PLANT-BASED ~~DIET~~ Living

This cookbook is vegan, but it is also WHOLE-FOODS, PLANT-BASED. If you're reading this, you probably already know what that means, but in case you don't, here's the gist.

*(I'm not fond of abbreviations, but whole-foods, plant based is a mouthful, so you'll see WFPB throughout this book. We also use SAD for standard American diet.):*

WFPB means eating a wide variety of minimally processed foods. On the "in" list are grains, vegetables, legumes (beans), tubers (yams), seeds, nuts, fruits, tofu, whole-grain breads and pastas, and plant-based milks. On the "out" list are pretty much all other processed foods, especially those with white flour, white rice, artificial flavors and sweeteners, added fat, and of course all meat and dairy.

I do not refer to this as a diet. The word *diet* has morphed into meaning a food strategy designed to lose weight. If you are currently using the SAD eating strategy, you will absolutely lose weight eating WFPB. But that is not what WFPB is all about. WFPB is about maximum health and vitality.

## VEGAN VS. WHOLE-FOODS, PLANT-BASED

Vegan and WFPB are often synonymous, yet different beasts. Vegan means no animal products. So, go to the burger joint and live on sodas and fries and *¡presto!* you are vegan. You might not live long, but you will be a vegan. WFPB is always vegan, in the sense of eating no animal products, but it adheres to more uptight health standards. You can be a junk-food vegan or a healthy-food vegan. But you can't be a junk food WFPB.

## THERE ARE OTHER REASONS NOT TO EAT THE ANIMALS

I'm WFPB primarily for health reasons. However, the humanitarian and environmental reasons are certainly a consideration. The longer I eat this way, the more important these issues become to me.

# HEALTH BENEFITS OF WFPB EATING

Proponents of WFPB believe in its potential to prevent and reverse a long list of problems, including but certainly not limited to heart disease, diabetes, obesity, high cholesterol, high blood pressure, cancer, and depression. This sounds like the list snake oil once *cured*, but the scientific evidence for WFPB is compelling, if not also self-evident and logical.

## THE OPPOSITE OF SICK + FAT

A quarter of Americans alive today will die of heart disease, according to Centers for Disease Control statistics. Millions more live with diminished health of some sort or another, which makes everyday living rough or restricted. Those of us lucky enough not to have a "condition" still feel lethargic and off some days. A lot of this is preventable with what we eat, or so say a new wave of physicians, such as Dr. Michael Greger, Dr. Caldwell Esselstyn, and Dr. T. Colin Campbell. They base their claims on credible independent scientific studies and personal observations from their own practices.

## BUT WHAT ABOUT PROTEIN, CALCIUM, AND AMINO ACIDS?

It's hard to toss out our diet assumptions, like protein must come from animals, or that milk prevents osteoporosis. But Dr. Greger and others are challenging these decades-old health relics — most notably by illuminating that the studies which *proved* such to be true were, in fact, faulty. These notions are so ingrained in our psyche that it's difficult to stop believing them.

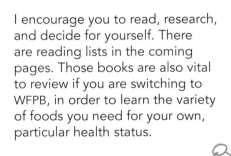

I encourage you to read, research, and decide for yourself. There are reading lists in the coming pages. Those books are also vital to review if you are switching to WFPB, in order to learn the variety of foods you need for your own, particular health status.

# GETTING STARTED ON WFPB

## RETHINKING LIFE'S PRIORITIES IS A GOOD PLACE TO BEGIN

We are all likely to get bad news from a doctor someday. I want that day to be a long way off. When I pondered what matters to me, the notion that arose was that the most important thing I can do for my family is to be healthy. Same for myself. I certainly don't want to have physical restrictions before my time. I don't mind growing older, but I don't want to start feeling old.

I definitely don't want to be the cause of my own disabilities and death.

## A SNOWBALL'S MOMENTUM ON A WILD RIDE

It starts small and builds quickly. Eating well gives you more energy. More energy gives you more motivation. More motivation gets you doing other things. Things like exercise and large projects you have been putting off. You start accomplishing more. This feels good, so you up your eating game. The snowball builds.

## BEING REALISTIC ABOUT CHANGE

I have seen a lot of information about the fantastic benefits of WFPB in just the first two weeks. I totally believe that the improvements in blood work and other health indicators are drastically influenced in that time, and that many people suddenly feel better and notice large changes. However, for me that was not the case. My blood work probably showed great improvement, but I didn't check. What I did notice was that I didn't notice any improvement in mood or energy during that time. But, I also already felt pretty good when I started WFPB (my primary goal at the time was to get my cholesterol and fasting glucose down without drugs).

I was a little disappointed that I didn't get this super boost I had read about. After eating crap for 60-plus years, I needed a lot more time than two weeks to feel a big difference. I have noticed an improvement in my energy, motivation, and mood over the first 18 months of going on WFPB. So, keep this in mind if you are expecting fantastic changes in two weeks, that may or may not be the case.

# SPECIFICS FOR STAYING THE COURSE

This does take time. Not weeks in a hospital recovering from heart surgery or a diabetic amputation, but still, it takes some effort to prepare most of your own food. This cookbook is all about how to minimize that time.

## SIMPLIFY

To stay on this eating style I need recipes that are simple. If a recipe calls for two or three mixing bowls, I'll try doing it all in one. If some fancy mushroom pops up on the ingredient list, I'll use regular button mushrooms. If one demands three types of flours, I'll just use whatever flour I keep in stock. In this book, I try to keep the complications and oddities to a minimum, but if you are just embarking on WFPB, you will need to pick up a few strange items. We'll tell you about those in the ingredient list section, just before the recipes start.

## ALWAYS HAVE SOMETHING READY TO EAT

Plan, so that when you get hungry, you have food readily available. If fast-food joints start to smell enticing, eat your pre-planned food pronto. Willpower can work for a span, but will eventually let you down, so don't count on it alone. Brown bag it to work. And don't keep rubbish in your house. We end up with piles of candy and other junk in the house around holidays. I encourage guests to take it with them, or toss it out as soon as everyone leaves.

## COOKING FRENZY

I make large batches of several recipes. It's heck on the kitchen but I end up with lots of ready-to-eat food in the refrigerator and freezer. I try to keep legumes ready to eat, so I may cook up a batch of sloppy Joe, barbecue beans, or split pea with sweet potato stew. Might as well bake a few sweet potatoes while I am hanging around the kitchen. Fill up the bread machine and get it started. And, if I am especially motivated, make a dessert. It takes a little planning and a few hours, but I end up with a ton of food. Then if we do a vegetable frenzy before dinner one night, we have food for a week or more. (Except for cooked, unfrozen veggies, which are probably only good for three or four days.)

# HOW STRICT?

My belief is that one small serving of meat a week or every other week would be okay. At this writing I have not had any meat in more than three years, but I am considering adding a very small amount to my diet. My reasoning is that even though I take B12, there are likely other trace elements I am missing. However, this cookbook remains totally WFPB because you can get recipes with meat, added salt, sugar, and fat anywhere.

## PERFECTION. DO AS I SAY.

My wife and I like to picnic under a bridge by the railroad tracks and watch trains go by. We set up chairs and everything. The police have given us the opinion that this is a strange place to picnic, but so far they have not kicked us out. Anyway, we stop at Panera Bread for our picnic food. I get a vegetable sandwich and black bean soup. Not too bad, but not even vegan because they put some crumbly cheese in the sandwich, and I have no idea what's in the soup. But the real problem comes when we both ask for the chips and usually get a dessert. So, I am not 100-percent compliant. On the plus side, I discovered an app called *Happy Cow,* which shows restaurants with vegan option in the area. With that I discovered a restaurant near us called San Francisco Stir Fry. It was good. Probably lots of oil, but also lots of fresh veggies and brown rice. We may switch to going there on our way to the tracks. Not perfect, but an improvement.

## AVOIDING SAD – THE STANDARD AMERICAN DIET

The difficulty in the WFPB lifestyle isn't that you can't find plenty of good things to eat. The problem is that you are constantly bombarded with the SAD food strategy. On TV, driving down the road, at parties, restaurants, etcetera. Plus, if you don't live on one of the coasts, your friends think you have gone off the deep end. But after being SAD for 60-plus years, I went to WFPB cold turkey (without the turkey even). If I can do it, you can do it.

This lifestyle is not hard. It only appears hard because it is so different from SAD. With some planning, it isn't difficult to stay with it. The rewards are incalculable.

# SEX... I MEAN CIRCULATION... OKAY, I MEAN SEX

WFPB has been proven to be the best food strategy to improve circulation. Good circulation is a necessity to get and maintain an erection. Good circulation is also important for other parts of your body. For instance, your brain. So, you may be measuring things like blood pressure and cholesterol, but they are in turn giving you an indication of how well your circulatory system is working. Erectile dysfunction is a likely sign of clogged arteries. ED is considered by some doctors to stand for *early death*. So, do your arteries and brain a favor. And while you're at it, you can throw away that Viagra.

## BRAINWASHING... *can be good for your health*

To stay on WFPB, it helps to become a student of this eating method. On the next pages are the experts from whom we draw knowledge and inspiration. Study until you understand. Until you have the scientific facts to know how to change your health circumstances. Learn until you are convinced enough to weather the constant storm of media misinformation and corporate trickery. Now that I've learned enough to understand the scientific and self-evident benefits, when I read an article about how beef broth is the greatest thing since sliced bread, or going into ketosis for long periods is a good way to diet, it's easy for me to identify those claims as fads and falsehoods. I've effectively brainwashed myself to replace the misinformation brainwashing I've been bombarded with for most of my life.

WFPB!

### MOTIVATION

is like bathing. You can't do it once and then never do it again. You must repeat on a regular basis. So, keep reading and gathering information on WFPB food strategy.

# WHERE TO GET BRAINWASHED

## RECOMMENDED READS + THE GURUS OF WFPB

I have tried high-fat, low-fat, low-carb, high-carb, and god knows what else to maintain my weight and get my cholesterol down. After no long-term success, I'd read about another diet, which would convince me my current one stank. I'd jump ship and try the next, and then the next one after that.

I first listened to Dr. Michael Greger's *How Not to Die* on audiobook. After a few chapters I quit listening because, "Hey this guy is nuts if he thinks I am going to be this extreme." Several months later I ran out of books to listen to, so in desperation and boredom I gave Greger a second chance. This time, whole-foods, plant-based resonated with me as common sense. Dr. Greger convinced me, and his food advice is a major foundation of this book.

There are other wise WFPB pioneers and advocates, and each of them brings forth a depth of scientific research and knowledge unparalleled in any sort of health book I've ever seen. Each has slightly different approaches. Dr. Caldwell Esselstyn deals with heart patients the rest of the medical community has given up on (with incredible success). His recommendations are far stricter than his son Rip's, who toned it down a little. My food strategy more closely follows Rip's than his father's. Not because I believe they are better, but because Rip's allow for a little more leeway. If I had heart disease, I would follow Dr. Esselstyn's protocol.

Read, research, and make your own decisions on what works for you. The important thing is to take time to learn and make a thoughtful decision about what you eat. Your health is worth the time.

### Books

*How Not to Die,* by Dr. Michael Greger, M.D.
*Prevent and Reverse Heart Disease,* by Dr. Caldwell B. Esselstyn, Jr.
*The China Study,* by T. Colin Campbell, Ph.D. and Thomas M. Campbell II, M.D.
*The Starch Solution,* by John A. McDougall, M.D. and Mary McDougall
*Plant Strong,* by Rip Esselstyn
All of these authors also have pretty good cookbooks, too.

### Documentaries

*Forks Over Knives,* directed by Lee Fulkerson, 2011
*What the Health,* directed by Kip Andersen, 2017
*The Game Changers,* directed by Louie Psihoyos, 2018
*Dr. Gregor daily videos and blogs,* nutritionfacts.org

### Apps & websites

*Daily Dozen* Dr. Gregor's daily nutrition-tracking app
*Happy Cow,* app that shows restaurants with vegan options nearby
*easygoingWFPB.com,* our website with links and more recommendations

# FUNCTIONING IN PUBLIC

## DON'T TRY THIS IN CLEVELAND. (I KNOW, THAT'S WHERE I LIVE.)

I have had people say they would rather die than adopt my lifestyle. My thought to this is that my lifestyle is very enjoyable. The challenges are not a drudgery, but rather fun. I am never very hungry. I can eat as much as I like. I have more energy than ever. I feel great. This lifestyle, if followed by too many, would put many doctors out of business. So, if you would rather die, that's your problem, not mine.

Those are my thoughts. But I don't say them out loud much.

## WHEN I DO OPEN MY BIG MOUTH...

I wish I could follow my eating strategy without anyone knowing, caring, questioning my manhood, giving me advice on my need for protein, or just discussing it in general. The problem is that everyone eating a SAD diet knows they should be eating more fruits and vegetables and less meat. So, when someone points out my eating strategy, they usually also defend their shoddy eating strategy. If you argue with them, you just come off as holier than thou.

Speaking of preaching, it is hard to resist the urge to correct other people's bad eating strategies. You want what's best for your friends and loved ones, but they don't want to hear it. It is like being born again and wanting to spread the word of God. This cookbook is a prime example. I feel born again in that I have reshaped my eating habits and would like to show others the way. The problem begins when you try to convert someone who is not interested in converting. It's like someone knocking on your door and asking if you want to discuss Jesus. My response is no, I don't want to discuss Jesus. Go away! I don't have a problem spreading the word of WFPB in this book because I am preaching to people who want to hear the message. Amen.

## RESTAURANTS

Which brings me to another point. Apparently some WFPB people go to great extremes. For instance, calling restaurants before going and talking with the cook to prepare a special meal, or discussing with the server in detail about what they will or will not eat. I don't do that. When I eat out, I am a vegan. I assume the food will have too much salt, sugar, and fat. I assume that I can order side dishes that will be vegan, or ask for slight modifications, like a pizza with no cheese, or spaghetti with marinara sauce. That usually means crap noodles or crust, but I can live with that. If I can avoid discussing my food strategy with the waiter, that is a win for me.

## WHEN I MIGHT AS WELL BE A MARTIAN

When I must explain what my food strategy is, I say I am vegan. I use the word vegan, because to explain WFPB is too much to comprehend for the average person. Even vegan is usually too much. When someone asks if I am vegan, the typical next question is, "Do you eat eggs?" That will be followed by, "What about dairy?" "Where do you get your protein?" "Do you eat fish?" No way am I going to get the concept of WFPB with no added salt, sugar, or fat across. With that, I think most people in my town would step back slowly, and walk away.

It's not that people mean to be irritating. It's just that most have never heard of these ideas. But slowly, they seem to be working their way past the coasts and into the lexicon of American cuisine.

## DINNER PARTIES

I feel bad for people having dinner parties anymore. One person is vegan, another is Paleo, and another is gluten or nut free. What to serve?? I feel bad that I contribute to this dilemma. I wish people would just serve whatever they want and let me pick and choose what I will eat. I understand the desire to please everyone, but these days that just isn't always possible. I can always bring a dish to share that suits my "diet."

# INGREDIENTS
# & COOKING TIPS

I dig the carrot dogs.

# INGREDIENT BASICS

## ORGANIC + RAW

My recipes don't indicate that each ingredient is organic, raw, reduced salt, or whatever. I don't do that because it would make the list look daunting. But, assume:

- all nuts are raw and unsalted.
- all fruits and vegetables should be organic if possible. If not, don't sweat it. A non-organic veggie is still way better than a fast-food burger.
- all grains, flours, and noodles are whole grain.
- all ingredients should avoid added salt, sugar, and fat, or at least be low-salt, sugar, and fat versions if possible.
- for all canned food, try to get BPA-free. Cans have a plastic coating. I think BPA-free is best, but whatever they are using now will soon likely be discovered to emit something awful as well.

## TO ORGANIC OR NOT?

I prefer organic, but will do non-organic as long as the food is not on the Environmental Working Group's dirty dozen list (ewg.org). As for farmers' markets, they sound like a great idea, and have a nice, homey feel, but around here they rarely have organic produce and they always have candy, lousy baked goods, and in general have just not been helpful to me.

## STAINLESS COOKWARE, BLENDERS, + FOOD PROCESSORS

I use only stainless or glass cookware. Non-stick is controversial as to releasing fumes and other carcinogens. Fumes or no fumes, the non-stick cookware I have seen requires special spoons and spatulas, and should not be washed in the dishwasher. That's too much trouble. As for iron and aluminum, various studies of Alzheimer's patients show trace amounts of these elements in their brains. It's controversial, and it can be argued that the pans you use don't make much difference. But I don't see any reason for me to take a chance with my brain.

Some of my recipes use a blender. I have a high-speed blender. If you don't have a high-speed blender you can probably just blend for a longer time and get the same result, but I'm not sure of that. In any case, I would recommend having a high-speed blender. I also recommend a food processor.

# SHOPPING

Whole food is food that has been minimally processed without added or subtracted ingredients. White flour is wretched because the nutritious part of it has been removed. Whole-grain flour has been minimally processed, and so can be considered a whole food. Vegan milks are not whole foods, in that most their fiber has been removed. However, vegan milks are so much better than cow secretions, I consider them acceptable.

When shopping, I look for foods that are processed as little as possible. Obviously, this includes most fruits, vegetables, whole grains, dried legumes, and raw nuts. I also include some minimally processed foods like old-fashioned rolled oats, nut milks, canned beans, and spaghetti sauces. Prepared foods in a box, can, or bag are probably loaded with salt, sugar, fat, and chemicals that will not do your body any good. When I do buy these, I try to find the least processed ones, that are organic with no added salt, sugar, or oil. Meeting all those criteria is often not possible, but that is what I am looking for.

## WITH BEANS: TO COOK OR CRANK OPEN A CAN

I prefer to used dried beans, but sometimes I end up using canned beans for convenience. We have a hard time getting three servings of beans a day, so sometimes we buy canned baked beans. When we open them, we squeeze out as much of the liquid as possible. Hopefully that gets rid of most added ingredients. Probably not ideal, but it helps me get more servings of beans.

## COCOA VS. CACAO

Cocoa and cacao powder may be interchangeable in some recipes, but I always use cacao. Both are good for you, but cacao is better. Cocoa has been heated to a high temperature. Cacao has not, and has much higher concentrations of antioxidants. Cacao also has more fiber, magnesium and calcium. I have not compared the two for taste I just use cacao.

# GREEN LIGHTS

I like to think of foods as green light, yellow light, or red light. Green lights you can eat to your heart's content. Yellows are okay, but go easy on them. Reds should be avoided. However, it's okay to use red-light foods if you are using them to cause yourself to eat more green-light foods. For instance, hot sauce may have a lot of salt in it, so it would be a red-light food. But if you are using it to enhance the flavor of a green-light food like kale, then it's okay. I do use some yellow and red-light foods in this book, such as maple syrup, but very few, and only to enhance green-light foods.

## MAPLE SYRUP + DATE SUGAR

Maple syrup is probably just as bad as sugar, but in my opinion the health benefits of the ingredients I use it with outweigh the evil. I use date sugar and maple syrup for sweetener in recipes that call for sweeteners. Date sugar is not sugar. It is just ground up dates. So, it has all the fiber and nutrients that a date does. That makes date sugar a green-light food. If you have a sweetener you prefer, feel free to switch. I don't think the choice of a different sweetener to replace maple syrup would make much difference in most recipes. (The bread recipe is an exception. The salt and sweetener in that recipe must be measured very accurately to properly react with the yeast. Bread is the only recipe I use salt in. I tried reducing the salt to 1 teaspoon instead of 1 ½ teaspoons and the bread got very airy near the top of the loaf.)

## FAKE MEAT

When transitioning to WFPB from SAD, some people find it helpful to use fake meat. These substitutes are highly processed and probably not all that good for you, but they are an improvement over meat. I never cared for them, so I don't have much of an opinion on them. My meatloaf recipe is our meat stand-in. We use it as a substitute for ground meat, burger, and meatloaf.

## SEASONINGS

If you look at many seasoning mixes, like Italian or Cajun, salt will be near the beginning of the ingredients list, if not first. Watch out for that.

## CONDIMENTS

Condiments, for the most part, are not whole food and are loaded with salt, sugar, and/or fat. Pickles may be whole food, but usually have too much salt and sugar to be considered a high-quality food, unless they are fermented.

I have tried making my own condiments with better ingredients, but so far have failed to come up with any I am happy with. Since I am all about making it easy to follow WFPB, I just buy condiments. If the ketchup and mustard are organic, I am happy. As for hot sauce, I don't look at the ingredients. My assumption is that for the amount I am going to use, it just isn't that important.

I used to dip my French fried (baked, no oil) potatoes in ketchup, but now I have discovered I like mustard just as well. Organic mustard is, in my opinion, a good food. It has mustard, vinegar, and spices. With that in mind, I am using more mustard and less ketchup.

## IS IT WHOLE GRAIN?

Would advertisers try to mislead you? Food packaging is notorious. The words *whole grain* or *multi-grain* on a package don't mean a thing. Look for 100-percent whole grain. Without a percentage, *whole grain* could mean 1 percent.

I like following a general rule regarding carbohydrates versus dietary fiber. The carb content should be equal to or less than 5 times the fiber content. For instance, if the fiber content is 3 grams, the carbs should be 15 grams or less. The bread we buy at our local grocery store has 3 grams of fiber and 12 grams of carbs, so it fits the formula. This seems to be a good rule to follow (but also keep in mind overall content of other things, like salt, sugar, fat, etcetera).

### SPROUTED GRAINS

Another thing to look for in bread is sprouted grains. Sprouted-grain breads have less gluten and more nutrients. Ezekiel bread, in the frozen food section, is the only sprouted grain bread in my local store. As more research comes in, I assume more sprouted-grain breads will appear.

When shopping, keep in mind that *vegan* is the new advertising buzzword, and does not always equal *healthy*. It often means the manufacturer has swapped a few dairy or meat ingredients for a few non-meat and or non-dairy ingredients. Read the label.

# GREGER'S DAILY DOZEN

To ensure a balanced eating day, I use Dr. Greger's *Daily Dozen* app as a guideline. It lists his suggested ideal mix of foods. Would another of my favorite authors have slightly different recommendations? Sure. But I think they would all agree that this would be a heck of a good place to start. I don't follow the Daily Dozen religiously. But I do keep his guidelines in mind. By following the guidelines now and then, I learn my weaknesses. For instance, I have a hard time getting my greens. Without the app I wouldn't know that.

## DECODING SERVING SIZE

The app also spells out serving size. Just click the foods on the left side of the screen. If you clicked on greens, for example, it says one serving of greens is 1 cup raw or ½ cup cooked. Huh, 1 cup of greens? Is that loose? Tight? In-between? That doesn't help me much. But wait, there's more. If you tap units it will give you the measurement in grams. Okay, now with my $12 kitchen scale I can measure 60 grams. Now when I make my green smoothie, I know how much kale to put in the blender. I get about half of Dr. Greger's recommended greens with my smoothie.

Do I always measure it? Heck no. I rinse my kale and put it on a paper towel, scrunch it up and put it in the high-speed blender. I know by the size of the lump if I have the right amount. How close do I want to be? It's not important to be that close. For me, I don't want too much kale because then the smoothie will not taste good. I don't want too little because I want to get my greens. This is not a critical balance. Once you have an idea of what a serving is there is no need to always measure it.

*What is that in bushels, pecks, and pints?*

I try to get my green smoothie (p. 38) or anytime breakfast bowl (p. 37) in every day because they have several of the Daily Dozen I would have a hard time getting otherwise. For instance, turmeric and ground flaxseed. The Daily Dozen recommends ¼ teaspoon of turmeric and a tablespoon of ground flaxseed. So, I add those into my cereal or smoothie.

# EXPENSE

I don't know if WFPB is expensive. A better question might be how does the cost compare to a triple bypass? I have seen many articles on how WFPB can be done inexpensively, so I'm sure it can be done. But, not by me.

When I check out with a few pounds of organic raw cashews, walnuts, and dates, I can spend $50 to $100 and fit it all in one bag. My feeling on cost is that no matter how much extra I spend, it is cheaper than the cost of surgery, or a lifetime supply of drugs for diabetes, cholesterol, blood pressure, and who knows what else — not to mention a lowered quality of life.

Of course, some WFPB is less expensive. Grains and dried beans are cheap and easy to store. I have not fact checked this, but I assume many of my recipes are less expensive than the regular crap-food variations. For example, my WFPB meatloaf is probably cheaper than real meatloaf.

## VITAMINS

I'm not going to go into detail on vitamins (there's plenty of that in our recommended readings), but suffice it to say, substituting vitamins for whole food does not make a healthy diet. That being said, I do take some vitamins.

### B12

This is the one vitamin that is important to take on a WFPB food strategy. B12 is in dirt and animals. WFPB people would not need B12 if we ate plants with some dirt still on them, but our plants are cleaned too well, so we must supplement.

### D3

I live in Cleveland. We are not known as the sun capital. So, I take some D3.

### DHA/EPA FROM ALGAE

I also take DHA/EPA algae oil. There was a big news thing blathering on about how DHA does not stop heart disease, but they forgot to mention that there is still a lot of evidence it may help your brain.

### IODINE

Since I don't add salt to anything except my bread, I take a small amount of iodine. I probably don't need to, since I also (don't tell) eat in restaurants and am tempted by crap on occasion. My name is Tom, not St. Thomas.

# HOW TO USE THIS BOOK

For most recipes I have **THE ESSENTIALS** and **EXTRA DETAIL**.

## THE ESSENTIALS

The essentials are the basic nuts and bolts of the recipe. Once you've made the recipe, they are also designed to serve as a quick reminder for when you're jumping into it a second, third, or twelfth time. We've left blank spots near each recipe to encourage your notes and personalization.

## EXTRA DETAIL

When making a recipe for the first time, we encourage your use of the extra detail sections. They include optional ingredients, mistakes I've made while cooking, the power to overcome such faux pas, and tips on storage. It's probably a good idea to look at the extra detail the first time you make the recipe. After that, there may be no need to keep referring to it.

## AT THE VERY LEAST, TRY THESE – A.K.A. MY STAPLE RECIPES

Few recipes become favorites from any cookbook. However, I have a few that have become my everyday favorites. If you try any, I recommend these:

• Breakfast bowl (p. 37), kale veggie bean bowl (p.40), or kale-fruit-spices smoothie (p. 38) for their ease and nutritional blast.

• Mushroom stroganoff: this freezes well, it tastes great just by itself, and I can use it like gravy on veggies, noodles, bread, and rice (p. 56).

• Meatloaf: I make large batches and freeze it. It can be nuked and eaten plain, or cut up and used like ground meat in spaghetti and other dishes (p. 58).

• Baked beans: I am always trying to get plenty of beans and having this on hand makes it easy. I make it in large batches and freeze it in mugs. I can nuke it and eat it right out of the mug, or use it to top off a salad (p. 63).

• Split pea sweet potato soup: freezes well and is good all by itself (p. 78).

• Tri dressing: this lasts a long time in the refrigerator and has a lot of good ingredients. I use it on salads and sometimes I put a little on my cooked veggies. I also use it to dip raw veggies in when I don't have ranch dressing made (p. 81).

• Bread: I like the idea of using sprouted wheat bread but nothing in the grocery store does much for me. This bread I like (p. 94).

• Cashew rice. It's satisfying (p. 48).

## MY NOTES & OTHER FAVORITES

# SUPERFOODS

I am tired of hearing about the latest and greatest superfood. Rather than thinking, *gee I should get more so and so because it has lots of whatever in it*, I remind myself that just about any whole plant-based food could be written up as a superfood. All high-quality foods are superfoods. By the same token all crap food is crap.

# TASTE VERSUS HEALTH

I do not add kale to a smoothie to make it taste better. I add kale to make it easier for me to get my daily greens. I like my green smoothie, but I would probably like it better with a scoop of ice cream and no kale.

The average cookbook has recipes based entirely on how to get the best taste. The best way to do this is by adding copious amounts of fat, sugar, salt, and highly processed ingredients. If health is considered, it is usually following some absurd food pyramid or insane logic.

When I cook for others, I am torn between trying to come up with food that carnivores would like, and saying the heck with it. All food does not have to taste like butter, cheese, and meat. Get a grip. People on SAD or similar food strategies are rarely going to appreciate real food. Their taste buds are not going to adjust with one meal. They are not likely to be happy without the normal dose of salt, fat, sugar, dead animals, and cow secretions. So, if I am entertaining guests, I will try to come up with something suitable, but I will not fool myself with the thought that I am going to convince the SAD to be blown away by whatever I serve.

The recipes in this book are designed primarily to be healthful. If you are accustomed to recipes with animal flesh, cow secretions, salt, sugar, and fat, then some of the recipes will not taste familiar. If your primary goal is to enjoy the moment, you may prefer to stick with the SAD food strategy.

I am reminded of a saying by Zig Ziglar, "When you are tough on yourself, life is going to be infinitely easier on you."

# SHOPPING LIST

This is not a list of things to run out and get. It is just a list of things to look at sometimes before heading out to the grocery store. I recommend you make your own list and refer to it on occasion.

I would never have everything in stock. Looking at the list prior to shopping helps me remember items I may not have thought of otherwise.

When doing a cooking frenzy, I make a list of ingredients that I am about to run out of for my next shopping trip.

On your list, you may want to make a note of where you get some things. I use two different grocery stores and online. Certain things I like I can only get at one of those places. One of my stores is 10 miles away. So, when I go there, I want to stock up on the items that I can only find there.

### PRODUCE

apples
artichokes
avocados
bananas
broccoli
cabbage
carrots
cauliflower
celery
corn
cucumbers
garlic
kale
leafy greens
mushrooms
onions
oranges
pears
peppers
potatoes, sweet
potatoes, white, yellow, or red
spinach
tomatoes

### NUTS + SEEDS

almonds
Brazil nuts
cashews
chia seeds
flaxseed
pumpkin seeds
walnuts

### FROZEN FOOD

blueberries
cherries
corn
peas
rice

### BEANS (CANNED + DRIED)

baked, canned (vegetarian)
black
garbanzos
kidney
lentils
navy
split peas

## SPICES + CONDIMENTS

amla fruit powder
baking powder (no aluminum)
baking soda
barbecue sauce
bay leaves
Bragg liquid aminos
cacao (non-alkalized)
cinnamon (Ceylon)
chili powder
cornstarch
cumin
curry powder
cloves
date sugar
dill weed
flour (sprouted wheat)
ginger
hot sauce
ketchup
lemon juice
maple syrup
mustard (Dijon)
mustard (yellow)
mustard seeds (yellow)
nutritional yeast
nutmeg
onion powder
paprika (smoked)
parsley
pepper, black
pepper, cayenne
peppermint leaves
peppermint extract
pumpkin pie spice
tamari
thyme
Table Tasty (by Bensons)
turmeric
vanilla extract
vinegar, balsamic
vinegar, apple cider
Worcestershire sauce

## OTHER FOOD

bread (whole grain)
buns
dates (Medjool)
miso (I use Hikari)
non-dairy milk
oat bran
old-fashioned rolled oats
peanut butter
pasta, spaghetti (whole grain)
pasta, elbow (whole grain)
raisins
tomatoes (canned, diced)
tomato paste
tofu (silken and firm)

## MY NOTES + ADDITIONS

_____

_____

_____

_____

_____

_____

_____

# INGREDIENTS WORTH EXPLAINING

I tried not to put too many strange ingredients in here, but there are a few that deserve the trouble of trying them.

### AMLA FRUIT POWDER

Amla tastes awful. It has a very high antioxidant level. I mix a quarter teaspoon in my breakfast bowls and green smoothies, and then I don't notice the bad taste.

### CACAO

Cacao is a dry powder, like powdered baking cocoa. Cocoa is chocolate that has gone through more processing than cacao. For instance, cacao has not had any processing over 200 degrees F. Because of this reduced processing, cacao has more nutrients and antioxidants than cocoa. Many recipes could use either one, but I only use cacao in my recipes. In order to get organic cacao, I buy it online. For recipes that I cook, like chocolate muffins, the added nutritional value probably doesn't make any difference because of cooking them over 200 degrees.

### CHIA SEEDS

Chia seeds are high in nutrients, fiber, omega-3s, and make a great, super-easy-to-make pudding. The nutrients in chia seeds can be absorbed without grinding them. However, it is best to let them soak for an hour or so to be sure your body can process them.

### FLAXSEED (GROUND)

Like chia seeds, flaxseed is high in nutrients, fiber, and omega-3s. If eaten unground, the seeds will pass through your system and not do much good, so they should be ground up prior to using. Unground, the seeds will last a long time, but once ground they will spoil. Because of this you should grind your own. I recommend against buying ground flaxseeds in the store. Since ground flaxseed will spoil, I assume that store-bought ground ones have gone through some extra processing. Refrigerate after grinding.

### MISO

Miso gives food the taste benefits of salt without the downsides. The bad effects of the salt in the miso are offset by the good ingredients in the miso. For more on this, visit nutritionfacts.org. I have had very different results from different misos. So, I mention the one I use. This is not a recommendation, just a suggestion of what works for me. I use Hikari white miso.

### NUTRITIONAL YEAST

I use a lot of nutritional yeast. It adds a cheese-like flavor to things without the bad side effects of dairy products.

### TABLE TASTY

Table Tasty is a healthy salt alternative. It appears to be just a bunch of spices mixed together and ground very fine. The downside is that it is expensive, and if exposed to any moisture turns hard as a rock. I use it in two recipes, macaroni and cheese and fake Parmesan, both of which would be fine without it. But I like it.

# RECIPE ICONS

Use the icons on each recipe page for a shortcut to what you're seeking.

 Oven recipe

 Microwave recipe

 Stove-top recipe

 Blender or food processor

 Quick (under 20 minutes)

 Simple (just a few ingredients)

 Freezer-friendly for leftovers

 Snack for home

 Snack on the go

 Good car travel food

 Main course

 Sweet

 Carnivore guest might eat

# RECIPES & MEALS

# HAVING FOOD WHEN HUNGRY

## FREEZE 'EM FOR LATER

Try to stock your freezer with your food. My freezer always has bread, WFPB meatloaf, berries, and a variety of my recipes in mugs. The mugs I cover with wrap and label what they are, because sometimes I can't tell one from another when they are frozen. By doing this, I always have something I can heat and eat.

An important note on freezing things in mugs: if you nuke them on high to thaw them, the mug may break. I nuke them at 40 percent for 4 minutes, and then stir them and nuke on high for a little longer.

## I WANT TO EAT SOMETHING NOW, FAST FOOD IDEAS

When I started this journey, I would get hungry and have a hard time thinking of something to eat.

I assume you have already looked in the fridge and freezer. Glance at the table of contents for ideas. If that doesn't turn up any, here are a few:

Glance at the table of contents for ideas.

- Toast with nut butter, or just plain
  - Ants on a log, a.k.a nut butter on celery with raisins
- Fruit, dried or fresh
  - Nuts
  - Popcorn with nutritional yeast and Bragg's aminos
  - Veggies, raw or with ranch dressing, tri dressing, or bean dip
- Veggies, just raw by themselves
  - Can of veggies. This may sound strange, but eating a can of veggies right from the can is satisfying and convenient. It might not meet Julia Child standards, but who cares?

I consider all of my staple recipes, except tri dressing, as fast food because all I must do is nuke or toast them and they are ready to eat. My breakfasts are fast to make. Ants on a log are easy and quick. Sometimes I will nuke a white potato for a snack. And of course, fruits and veggies are always good fast food.

RECIPES

# TRIUMPHANT TRAVELING

## IDEAS THAT HAVE HELPED ME

I like coffee, and when I travel I find most places serve terrible coffee. I am not a bottled water fan, but for my morning joe I make an exception. I open a small bottle of water, drink a little, and dump a Starbucks instant coffee into it. Screw on the lid and shake. Not bad.

For each day I am going to be gone, I pack breakfast bowls and non-dairy milk in boxes from the non-refrigerated section.

We have a big cooler, which we load with three lidded plastic containers. We pack ice around them and stock them with fruits, veggies, sandwiches, and whatever. Every night, or every other night depending on the outside temperature, we pack new ice around the containers. (So we don't have to struggle to lift it all, we use a bag to cart the ice from the ice machine to the car). Voilà, a portable refrigerator.

Lots of restaurants have meals that are okay. The ones that I am familiar with are Starbucks and Chipotle Mexican Grill. At Starbucks I can get the oatmeal. It comes with little packets of nuts, raisins, and brown sugar. Yes, I use the sugar. I can't help myself. Chipotle is probably loaded with salt and fat, but I get the veggie bowl with brown rice and two kinds of beans. The Happy Cow app should also be helpful in finding suitable restaurants.

If we fly and are going to be gone for any period of time, we stop at a grocery store and hope motel rooms will have refrigerators in them.

RECIPES

# BREAKFAST (or anytime)

### MY 3 STANDARD MORNING MEALS

My three standard breakfasts are: anytime breakfast bowl (p. 37), kale, fruit, spice smoothie (p. 38), and the kale, veggie, bean bowl (p. 40). All three get me a lot of points on the Daily Dozen, and I like them. If I am in a hurry it will be the smoothie because I can take it with me in the car. I am also just as likely to have any one of these for lunch or dinner. I no longer think of certain foods as good for specific times of day. I think in terms of what will fill me up, be healthy, and easy.

breakfast bowl assembly line

# ANYTIME BREAKFAST BOWL

### INGREDIENTS

¼ cup old-fashioned rolled oats
¼ cup oat bran
¼ cup raisins
¼ teaspoon amla fruit powder
¼ teaspoon ginger
¼ teaspoon turmeric
1 tablespoon ground flaxseed
1 teaspoon Ceylon cinnamon
1 tablespoon date sugar
1 Brazil nut
small handful of walnuts
a bunch of blueberries
non-dairy milk to desired consistency

### THE ESSENTIALS

Put it in a bowl and eat.

### EXTRA DETAIL

It looks like a pain, but after you make your variation a few times, it only takes minutes. I keep a ¼ cup measure with my ingredients. My big bowl has about 29 grams of fiber, nearly twice what the average American gets in a day. It probably has more antioxidants than most SAD eaters get in a week.

Cinnamon: what you get from the local store is probably not Ceylon. Regular cinnamon has some things slightly poisonous in this quantity. If you don't have Ceylon, skip it.

Flaxseed: Ground flaxseed should be refrigerated. How it is sold in stores unrefrigerated, I cannot imagine. I recommend grinding your own. I don't like using a blender, so I dedicated a coffee grinder to the task, which keeps all the flaxseed the same consistency.

If I am not real hungry, I put some aside for later, before adding fruit and milk. Later I mix it with tea or water if I am not near almond milk. I use frozen berries, and sometimes nuke it for 30 seconds to thaw them. Amla powder tastes awful but is super high in antioxidants.

This is great for traveling. I premix a serving for each day I'll be gone and put them in Ziplock bags. Sometimes motels have nut milk. If not, I get boxes that don't have to be refrigerated until they're opened.

*\* For more information on the spices in this recipe, refer to the website nutritionfacts.org.*

# SMOOTHIE, KALE, FRUIT, SPICES

## INGREDIENTS
½ cup cherries
½ cup blueberries
1½ ounces kale
a few nuts
2 or 3 tablespoons peppermint leaves, dried
4 Medjool dates
¼ teaspoon ginger
1 tablespoon ground flaxseed
¼ teaspoon amla fruit powder
almond milk

## THE ESSENTIALS
Mix in a high-speed blender for 45 seconds.

## EXTRA DETAIL

I didn't put a lot of smoothie recipes in my cookbook because healthy smoothies are easy to find and dream up. I put in this one, and the fruit smoothie on page 43, because they are the ones I tend to make. This makes a big smoothie. I pour mine into a 24-ounce Mason jar. I drink it with a large straw to keep it out of my mustache.

Some experts think smoothies are good, some think they are bad. On the good side, the high-speed blending makes more of the nutrients available. On the downside, high-speed blending damages the fiber, plus it is easier to overload on calories when drinking your calories. I like smoothies. They help me get a lot of nutrients and greens. I drink them slowly, so they don't spike my blood sugar.

## TROUBLESHOOTING

This drink is already thicker than I like without the flaxseed, so I put the flaxseed on top and eat it with a spoon, mixed with a little of the smoothie. If I put ground flaxseeds into my mixer, they stick to the side and make it very hard to rinse out. So, I pour my smoothie into a mason jar. Then I add the ground flaxseed. The ground flaxseeds do not stick to the mason jar. My blender has plastic containers. If yours has glass this is probably not a consideration.

Update: I stopped at a fancy kitchen supply store and looked at high-speed blenders. They were all plastic.

# KALE, VEGGIE, BEAN BOWL

## HOT OR COLD

### INGREDIENTS
2 to 4 large kale leaves, finely cut with scissors
handful of cauliflower and broccoli, diced
beans, baked beans, or peas
tri dressing
few walnuts
pepper
⅛ teaspoon turmeric

### THE ESSENTIALS
Rinse, dry, and cut kale into small pieces with scissors into a bowl.
Cover with chopped cauliflower and broccoli.
Add beans and dressing. Toss.

### EXTRA DETAIL
Don't let the name fool you. This is just a tossed salad. Open your fridge and add
whatever looks good.

Some things I typically add:

onions
celery
tomatoes
spinach
white potatoes
any veggie frenzy leftovers

RECIPES

BREAKFAST

## HOT OR COLD?

You decide. If you are going to have it cold, you will have to use a bigger bowl, so you have room to toss it. If you are going to heat it up, the kale will shrink quite a bit, which gives you some extra room. A heated tossed salad may sound strange but is good, just different. To heat, stick it in the microwave for 60 seconds. When it shrinks, it's done.

Add your favorite fat-free dressing and enjoy. I always use my tri dressing. I cut my veggies and kale up small enough to eat with fork, or sometimes a spoon. It looks strange, but I like it. If you're doing Dr. Greger's Daily Dozen this is worth 5 points.

I add the turmeric, nuts, and pepper because Dr. Greger touts that combination as having lots of antioxidant properties. Also, I like the taste.

## MORE DETAIL ON KALE

Previously I could never stand kale. Then I signed up for some farmer thing that delivered produce to my house. One day they delivered kale. Well, I couldn't stand to just throw it away, so I ate it and didn't die. With time I learned more about how to prepare it, and now I like it. I am going to tell you how I store it and prepare it. I have heard of chefs kneading it and other ways, so mess around and come up with your own methods, too.

When I bring kale home, I take it out of the bag, put some water on it, and put it back in the bag. My logic is that grocery stores mist their produce. If keeping the produce wet works for them, I figure it will work for me. If I have a lot of kale and want it to last more than a week, I wet it and put it in a large Ziplock bag. I squeeze the air out, close the bag, and wrap a rubber band around it to keep it from trying to expand and suck in air. I have tried fancy bags and egg things that supposedly make produce last longer, but have not had great luck with that. I probably didn't pay attention to the directions, but whatever. This system works for me.

When I use the kale, I rinse each leaf individually. Then, I hold the stem in one hand and with the other I lightly surround the stem and strip off the leaf. I collect the kale on a paper towel. When I have the amount I want, I scrunch it up to dry it off a little. If I am making a smoothie, I remove the paper towel and stuff the kale into a blender. (*Cat owner tip: I put the paper towel on the counter to dry for picking up cat barf later.*) If I am making a salad, I keep the kale in a tight ball and start cutting off small bits of it into a bowl. I cut it so small that a lot of times I eat my salad with a spoon. During all these processes, be rough with the kale. Kale is not delicate like lettuce or spinach. The rougher you treat it, the more tender it will become.

Kale may not taste good by itself. However, just like iceberg lettuce, people typically don't eat it by itself. I use it in sandwiches, salads, and smoothies. When used appropriately, it is good.

RECIPES

BREAKFAST

## Some more breakfast ideas...

# BEGINNER BREAKFAST BOWL

### INGREDIENTS
½ cup old-fashioned rolled oats
1 heaping tablespoon oat bran
⅔ cup boiling water
¼ cup raisins
¼ cup broken walnut pieces
non-dairy milk

### THE ESSENTIALS
Nuke or boil the water, stir it into the oats and oat bran. Top with fruit, nuts, and non-dairy milk.

### EXTRA DETAIL
This is my wife Kib's typical breakfast. Also consider assorted berries (fresh or frozen), Ceylon cinnamon, and sliced bananas.

RECIPES

BREAKFAST

beginner ↑

with non-dairy milk ↖

# SMOOTHIE, FRUIT

## INGREDIENTS

½ cup cherries
½ cup blueberries or a banana
½ tablespoon cacao
3 tablespoons spearmint leaves, dried
1 tablespoon date sugar
1 to 1½ cups almond milk

## THE ESSENTIALS

Blend.

## EXTRA DETAIL

For cherries and blueberries, I used frozen.

# MAIN COURSES

# BARBECUE PULLED PORK (WFPB of course)

### INGREDIENTS
1 head of red cabbage, chopped or grated
1 to 2 onions, diced
a few celery stalks, diced
1 cup barbecue sauce (I use Bone Suckin' Sauce)
1 tablespoon chili paste or hot sauce

### THE ESSENTIALS
Sauté the cabbage, onions, and celery in a large pot until all of the liquid is removed. Add the barbecue sauce and simmer for 5 to 10 minutes.

### EXTRA DETAIL
A chopped head of cabbage takes a very large pot. Even if you make a half recipe, it takes a large pan to cook the cabbage down.

I use a little sherry for some liquid to start the sautéing, but water would do or just cook it down slowly.

I use red cabbage because red cabbage has more antioxidants than green.

It does take a lot of barbecue sauce. One cup would be enough for a small head of cabbage, but I keep adding sauce until I feel the amount is right.

I freeze this in mugs and can make two sandwiches from one mug. I also eat it right out of the mug.

# BLACK BEANS & RICE

## INGREDIENTS
1 can black beans, 15 ounces, not drained
       (or whatever canned beans you have handy)
2 cups rice (we use one bag of frozen organic brown)
⅛ cup sherry, optional
½ cup diced green olives, omit if you want to be super healthy
1 cup frozen corn, optional

## TOPPINGS WE LIKE
onions
cucumbers, diced
tomatoes, diced
hot sauce

## THE ESSENTIALS
Heat the beans with their liquid, sherry, olives, and corn in a pan. Serve in bowls over rice.

## EXTRA DETAIL
We nuke the rice in a covered Corningware dish, or just heat it in the bag it comes in. This makes an almost instant meal.

# BURGERS (see meatloaf)

### BURGERS... THAT DON'T FALL APART
If you have leftover meatloaf WFPB from page 58, a slice of that makes a good hamburger.

If you want to look like a normal person at a picnic... instead of putting the mixture in a loaf pan, form it into burger patties and put them on parchment paper on a cookie sheet. Bake at 350 degrees for 12 to 15 minutes each side. Make them up ahead of time and freeze them.

RECIPES

MAIN COURSES

# CASHEW RICE

### INGREDIENTS
2 celery stalks, chopped
½ onion, chopped
2 garlic cloves, diced
2 cups cooked wild or brown rice
1 cup raw cashews, coarsely chopped
½ teaspoon thyme
½ teaspoon nutmeg
1 bunch parsley, chopped (fresh if you have, or 1 tablespoon dried)
serve with Bragg's spray amino, soy sauce, or tamari

### THE ESSENTIALS
Sauté celery, onions, and garlic. Add everything and mix.

### EXTRA DETAIL
We buy frozen ready-to-eat brown rice for this recipe.

# CHILI

## INGREDIENTS

1 onion, diced
1 can diced tomatoes with juice, 28 ounces
3 cans beans with juice, kidney, pinto, black, or mix and match, 15 ounces each
2 tablespoons chili powder
optional additions:
        hot sauce
        corn
        green olives, diced
        crumbled meatloaf from page 58

## THE ESSENTIALS

Sauté onion. Add everything else and heat and serve, or let simmer for 30 minutes.

# CREAM SAUCE

## WITHOUT TOFU

½ cup raw cashews
1 cup water
1 tablespoon flour or cornstarch

## WITH TOFU

½ cup raw cashews
1 cup water
1 pound silken tofu
1 tablespoon flour or cornstarch

## THE ESSENTIALS

Use cornstarch for sweet sauces, flour for gravies and non-sweet sauces. By itself this tastes bland. Add sweet ingredients and you have a sweet sauce for puddings and fruit. Add spicy ingredients and get a main course.
Use your imagination as to what to add, or keep reading for some ideas.

## EXTRA DETAIL

A cream sauce can make most anything into a decadent comfort food.
Cream sauces are basically a starch added to a liquid. When I was growing up the ingredients were white flour, cow milk, and butter. Most SAD cream sauces today have the same basic ingredients. My cream sauces use only healthy ingredients, and are just as good.

There are two ways to heat up cream sauce:

*I.* Heat it up with the flour already in. If I am going to blend my sauce in a blender, I add the flour to the blender. The advantage of this way is that the flour is super mixed in, with no chance of getting lumps, and you may end up with leftover sauce to use later. The disadvantage is that you have to stir or whisk constantly while bringing the sauce to a boil.

*2.* Mix the flour with a little water and add it to the already boiling liquid. The advantage to this way is that you don't have to stir or whisk as much, and you get just the right amount of cream sauce. The disadvantage is that you may get lumps, but not if you do it right. The trick is to put the flour in a cup and slowly add water while stirring vigorously. It is ready when you get enough water to have a liquid instead of a paste. When you add it to the hot cream sauce, give it a final quick stir, then stir the sauce vigorously as you add the mixture. Stop adding when the sauce is a consistency you like.

**DANGER:** Cream sauce makes big burps when it boils, and will splat hot goo all over the stove and you if you are not careful. As the sauce starts to thicken, stir rapidly until you take it off the stove. If the sauce is burping too much, it is probably too thick and needs more liquid.

# CREAM SAUCE IDEAS

In addition to having only healthy ingredients in this cream sauce, you can make it sweet for dessert-type things. Or, add stuff like miso or pepper to make main courses

## TOFU

The sauce is very much the same with or without tofu. I like to use the tofu to get more protein in my food. I know, that shouldn't be an issue, but after 70 years of being told I need protein, I can't help myself.

## IDEAS OF THINGS TO ADD TO THE SAUCE FOR COMFORT MAIN DISHES

miso
Worcestershire sauce
hot sauce
tamari
pepper

## IDEAS FOR PUDDINGS & SWEET SAUCES

For puddings, make the cream sauce thicker than normal, then try:
Medjool dates (added in blender)
sweetener of your choice
Ceylon cinnamon
vanilla
cacao

## EXPERIMENT

You will see this recipe used in several recipes in this book:
creamed turnips (p. 65)
stroganoff (p. 66)
vanilla and chocolate puddings (p. 91 and 89)

NOTE: my recipes call for a little more flour than is needed because it is easier to add more liquid to get the consistency I want than to add more flour or cornstarch.

ANOTHER NOTE: Sometimes when thawing frozen cream sauces, there may be some separation. If you want it just right for company, it is safest to make it when needed. I use thawed cream sauces all the time and don't have a problem with the slight change. You may not agree.

RECIPES

MAIN COURSES

# CREAMED VEGGIES, RICE, PASTA

## INGREDIENTS

½ cup raw cashews
1 cup water
1 tablespoon soy or tamari
1 pound silken tofu
2 tablespoons lemon juice
2 teaspoons Worcestershire
2 tablespoons miso
1 tablespoon parsley
2 tablespoons nutritional yeast
1 tablespoon flour

## THE ESSENTIALS

Put all of the above ingredients into a high-speed blender and blend for 45 seconds. Put in a pan and bring to a boil, whisking constantly until thickened. Add precooked veggies, rice, or pasta and continue stirring until hot. Or, make the sauce, then pour over veggies, pasta, or rice.

## EXTRA DETAIL

It will be too thick. This is on purpose, because it is easier to add water or non-dairy milk than to add flour. Add liquid until you like the consistency. Add veggies and/or pasta until you like the goo-to-veggie ratio, or pour over your veggies, rice, or pasta.

Half the time my grocery store doesn't have silken tofu, so I have discovered that firm tofu works fine. You will need to add water to the blender. You may also need to add a little more water to get the consistency you would like.

Cooking variation: If you don't put the flour in the blender, the sauce will be less likely to splat hot liquid while heating. You can't just add the flour to the hot liquid because it will make lumps and not mix in. So, put the flour in a cup and add small amount of liquid while stirring vigorously. Add just enough liquid to get a watery liquid. Now add that slowly to the sauce while stirring rapidly. Careful, the sauce will thicken quickly and start to spurt.

RECIPES

MAIN COURSES

# HOT DOGS ... *psst, it's a carrot*

## INGREDIENTS
carrots
hot dog buns or wraps (whole grain)
your condiments of choice

## THE ESSENTIALS
Scrub the carrots. I don't bother peeling them. Boil until fork soft, about 10 minutes. Cut in half lengthwise. Put two halves in a bun with the thick ends opposite each other. Add your condiments and dig in.

## EXTRA DETAIL
I make extras and refrigerate them. They make good dogs the next day. I don't even bother to reheat them. I have read that some chefs peel the carrots to get rid if the bitter taste, but I never noticed that, and figure lots of the vitamins are in the skin. I just brush the carrots clean and cut off the ends before boiling. Put your normal condiments on them. These are hit at a picnic even with the carnivores. Possible fixings: mustard, ketchup, kale, raw onions, caramelized onions, jalapeños, sauerkraut, or whatever you would put on a hot dog made from animal carcasses.

# LENTIL STEW OR SLOPPY JOE

## INGREDIENTS

2 ½ cups veggie broth or water
1 large onion
1 bell pepper, diced
1 tablespoon chili powder
1 ½ cups dried lentils
1 can diced tomatoes, 15-ounces
2 tablespoons tamari
1 tablespoon maple syrup
1 tablespoon vinegar
1 tablespoon Worcestershire
1 tablespoon parsley
pepper

## THE ESSENTIALS

Put everything in a pot, bring to a boil, simmer for 60 to 90 minutes. If you are using this for stew, it is okay to add a little extra liquid to get the consistency you would like.

## EXTRA DETAIL

When I put this on a bun, I call it a sloppy Joe. When I put it on bread, I call it an open-faced sloppy Joe. When I have it by itself, I call it lentil stew. It is a little mushy for a regular sloppy Joe on a bun, but if the buns are soft, it still works. I also put this on baked white potatoes. I usually freeze most of it in mugs.

open-faced sloppy Joe

RECIPES

MAIN COURSES

# MACARONI & CHEESE

**INGREDIENTS: Mac & Cheese Powder**
1 cup cashews
¾ cup nutritional yeast
½ cup whole-wheat flour
1 tablespoon paprika
2 teaspoons Table Tasty

**INGREDIENTS: The Mac & Cheese**
1 cup mac & cheese powder (above)
box of elbow noodles, 8-ounces
¼ cup miso (about 2 globs)
2 cups non-dairy milk
(add more as needed for consistency)
peas or any vegetables handy, optional

### THE ESSENTIALS
Process the dry cheese powder ingredients in a food processor for 2 to 3 minutes. Cook the elbows, drain and put aside. Use the pan you boiled the noodles in, whisk the milk, mac and cheese powder, and miso together, adding milk until you have a consistency you like. Dump the noodles in, and peas if you like. If using frozen peas, keep cooking until they are warmed up.

### EXTRA DETAIL
Put the dry ingredients in a food processor for 2 to 3 minutes. This powder can be saved to make mac and cheese anytime. I store mine in a mason jar. To make the sauce, I put about a cup of the powder in a pan with a couple of big globs of miso, then whisk it together with almond milk. Bring it to a boil while whisking a lot, and adding more milk or powder to get the thickness you like. Add your previously prepared elbow noodles. I like a high goo-to-elbows ratio. If this is too much goo for you, add chopped-up veggies until the goo ratio is one you are happy with. I like to add peas.

I put the cooked elbows in a colander and leave them there while I use the same pan to mix the mac and cheese. I have seen this recipe call for ¼ cup of oat flour and ¼ cup of tapioca flour instead of ½ cup whole-wheat flower. This does make a slightly better-looking dish and may have a slightly better consistency, but I wouldn't bother buying strange flours unless you are trying to avoid wheat or are pickier that I am.

Refrigerated leftovers will get much thicker and need more milk when heating.

# MUSHROOM STROGANOFF OR STROGANOFF GRAVY

## INGREDIENTS

1 diced onion

1 pound sliced mushrooms
  *or ½ pound cooked down*

½ cup raw cashews

1 cup water

1 tablespoon soy or tamari

1 pound silken tofu
  *or if you have firm on hand, that will
  work, just add more water*

1 tablespoon lemon juice

1 tablespoon Worcestershire

2 tablespoons miso

1 tablespoon parsley

2 tablespoons nutritional yeast

1 tablespoon flour

## THE ESSENTIALS

Sauté the onion and mushrooms slowly until most of the liquid is gone. While that's sautéing, blend the other ingredients in a high-speed blender for 45 seconds. Put everything together and bring to a boil, whisking or stirring constantly. Use like gravy, serve on bread, white potatoes, rice, noodles, or veggies.

## EXTRA DETAIL

This recipe has a high goo-to-mushroom ratio, which I like. If you prefer a lower goo-to-mushroom ratio, start with more mushrooms or add a veggie like corn or peas. At first it will be too thick. This is on purpose because it is easier to add water or non-dairy milk than to add flour. Add liquid until you like the consistency.

Firm tofu works fine, but you will just need to add a little more water or non-dairy milk to get the consistency you like.

You could probably substitute any non-dairy milk for the water and cashews if you don't have cashews on hand, but I have not tested that idea.

# RICE & VEGGIES

## INGREDIENTS
brown rice, we usually use frozen from a box
veggies, we usually use frozen corn and peas
mushrooms, if you happen to have some cooked up
tamari to taste, optional
pepper, optional
hot sauce, optional

## THE ESSENTIALS
We put the rice, veggies, and mushrooms in a covered microwavable dish and nuke.

# MEATLOAF

## YES, IT'S WFPB, AND SO WORTH THE EFFORT

### INGREDIENTS
2 celery stalks, diced
½ onion, diced
10 ounces firm tofu
¼ cup chopped walnuts
2 cups cooked lentils
    ¾ cup dry lentils
    1¼ cups water
    cook until liquid absorbed
1 cup old-fashioned rolled oats
3 tablespoons tamari
1 tablespoon Dijon mustard
2 teaspoons parsley

### THE ESSENTIALS
Sauté the celery and onions in water or wine a little. Throw the walnuts into
the sauté pan and everything else into the food processor. My food processor,
a Braun, has a dull plastic blade and a sharp metal blade. For this recipe I like
to use the dull plastic blade, but the sharp one also works fine. Just process
enough that the lentils get mushed and the tofu evenly mixed. Then add the
contents of the sauté pan. If you are using a sharp blade in your food processor,
mix the onions, nuts, and celery in by hand. Put in a lightly oiled loaf pan and
bake at 350 degrees for 60 minutes

### EXTRA DETAIL
I make a triple batch of this on a regular basis. After it cools, I slice it up and put
it on plates, interleaved with wax paper, and freeze it. Once frozen, I remove
the plates to save a little freezer room.

To oil the loaf pan, I put a little olive oil in the pan and wipe it all around with
a paper towel. Then I take a second paper towel and wipe out as much as
possible.

RECIPES

MAIN COURSES

# GROUND MEAT SUBSTITUTE
## (see meatloaf)

### GROUND MEAT SUBSTITUTE
To make ground meat substitute, dice up and crumble a few slices of meatloaf (WFPB) from page 58.

# SPAGHETTI

### INGREDIENTS
1 jar store-bought spaghetti sauce
1 pack noodles

### THE ESSENTIALS
Follow the directions.

### EXTRA DETAIL
Kib, my wife, likes to add crumbled WFPB meatloaf (page 58) and mushrooms to the sauce. I like to add lots of whatever vegetables are in the refrigerator and hot sauce. I like using Engine 2 sauce because it only has good ingredients. If a sauce is a little watery, I add some ground flaxseed to thicken it. Either way, put on top of whole-grain noodles and you have a healthy meal.

with meatloaf crumbles ↓                with no Parmesan ↓

with veggies ↑                with WFPB Parmesan ↑

RECIPES

MAIN COURSES

# TACOS

## INGREDIENTS
1 can black beans, drained, 15 ounces
1 cup pico de gallo or salsa, drained
1 ½ cups frozen corn
2 teaspoons chili powder
hot sauce
something to put it in, like a taco shell, romaine lettuce, or tortillas

## THE ESSENTIALS
Drain and rinse the beans in a sieve, use the same sieve to drain the corn if you're using canned corn, and use the same sieve to drain the pico de gallo or salsa. Mix together with the chili powder and hot sauce. Serve hot or cold.

## EXTRA DETAIL
The ingredient amounts aren't critical. One can of beans, one can of corn, one jar of salsa or pico de gallo. Or, if you're using frozen corn, use the empty bean can to measure the corn.

## GOOD ADDITIONS
jalapeños
avocado
kale

# SIDE DISHES, SOUPS & DRESSINGS

# BAKED BEANS

## INGREDIENTS
1 pound of dried great northern beans, soaked and cooked
1 to 2 onions, diced
1 can tomato paste, 6 ounces
1 tablespoon Worcestershire sauce
2 tablespoons molasses
2 tablespoons vinegar
2 tablespoons tamari
1 tablespoon mustard,
     yellow or Dijon
1 teaspoon smoked paprika
1 teaspoon liquid smoke
⅛ cup maple syrup
hot sauce to taste

## THE ESSENTIALS
Put in covered oven-safe pot and bake at 350 degrees for 60 to 90 minutes. I add the hot sauce after it is cooked.
That way I can better judge how much to add.

## EXTRA DETAIL
Great northern beans are best. Pinto beans are okay. I didn't care for black beans in this recipe. One pound of dried beans equals about 6 cups of cooked or 4 cans of rinsed beans.

## HOW I PREPARE BEANS FROM DRIED

Soak for 6 to 12 hours and drain. The soak removes most of the lectins that are bad. Rinse, drain, and re-add water. Simmer approximately 45 to 60 minutes until the beans are the consistency you like. I rinse and drain the beans again on the assumption I am getting rid of more lectins.

# BEETS

### INGREDIENTS
beets

### THE ESSENTIALS
Cover with water and boil for about 45 minutes until a fork sticks in them easily.

While running under cold water, scrunch them with your hands to remove the skin.

Rinse and cut off a little bit of the ends.

### EXTRA DETAIL
If the beets have greens on them, cut the greens off, rinse, and strip off the stalks. Steam the greens for 5 to 6 minutes.

Beet greens are very good for you, but I don't use them very much. Unless they are big and clean, they take a lot of time to rinse.

I cook 3 to 6 beets at a time, then cut the big ones in half and put them all in a bowl to refrigerate.

just beets ↑

with beet greens ↑

RECIPES

SIDE DISHES

# CREAMED TURNIPS

## INGREDIENTS
¼ cup raw cashews
1 cup water
1 pound turnips
1 tablespoon flour
2 tablespoons miso

## THE ESSENTIALS
Peel and cut turnips into quarters and boil for 10 to 15 minutes until fork soft. Don't overdo it and make them mushy.

Cut up the turnips into about dime-sized pieces.

Blend the cashews, water, miso, and flour in a high-speed blender for 45 seconds.

Bring the sauce to a boil, stirring constantly. It will get a little too thick, so add water to get the consistency you would like, then add the turnips.

## EXTRA DETAIL
When this starts to boil it will want to burp and splatter. Stir or whisk constantly to prevent this, and turn the heat down if needed.

This recipe works well with lots of other cooked veggies. I used creamed turnips because it was one of my father's favorite dishes.

# FRENCH FRIES (*not fried*)

### INGREDIENTS
sweet or white potatoes

### THE ESSENTIALS
Clean but don't peel. Cut into thick fries, ¾ to 1 inch (sure, ¼ inch would be nice as well, but why bother?). For all but the largest potatoes, I just quarter them lengthwise. Place on parchment-paper-covered cookie sheet. Put the potato skin side down. Bake at 450 degrees for 45 minutes.

### EXTRA DETAIL
If you would like, you can sprinkle the potatoes with seasoning before cooking. On white potatoes, consider chili powder, pepper, rosemary, or smoked paprika. On sweet potatoes, consider nutmeg, pumpkin spice, or date sugar. The potatoes are good with or without the spices. I serve the white potatoes with ketchup and/or mustard, depending on how I feel.

sweet ↑                    white ↖

### SPEAKING OF WHITE POTATOES...

Some experts like white potatoes, others don't. Read the books and you decide. I consider them a green-light food.

# KALE

## INGREDIENTS
kale

## THE ESSENTIALS
Hold the leaf firmly in one hand, stem in the other hand, pull to separate, and rinse.
Boil with a little water in a covered pan for 4 to 6 minutes, or steam it.
Save any leftover water for veggie broth.

## EXTRA DETAIL
I do it in large bunches.

After it cools, I bag it in baggies and freeze them. I like kale as a side-dish veggie with my tri dressing.

If possible, when you eat kale or any cruciferous veggie that has been cooked, add a few drops of balsamic vinegar or mustard powder to reconstitute the nutrients.

RECIPES

SIDE DISHES

# MASHED POTATOES

### INGREDIENTS
2 pounds white potatoes, scrubbed and cut into quarters
2 tablespoons miso
nut milk, added to the consistency you like
pepper

### THE ESSENTIALS
Boil the potatoes about 25 minutes until fork soft.
Mash with miso and nut milk.
I leave the skins on.

RECIPES

SIDE DISHES

# MASHED POTATO SLOP

## MY WIFE, KIB, ARGUED FOR A BETTER TITLE*

### INGREDIENTS
any leftover mashed potatoes
any leftovers from veggie frenzy
frozen corn or peas
more non-dairy milk
chopped-up WFPB meatloaf, if you have it
pepper
hot sauce

### THE ESSENTIALS
Mix and heat into a thick soup. Add whatever you have on hand that sounds good.

This is one of my favorites.

\*
Maybe Mashed Potato Ragout?
Or Soup? She offered.
But I stubbornly insisted on calling it Slop.

# MUSHROOMS

### INGREDIENTS
mushrooms, sliced
teriyaki sauce

### THE ESSENTIALS
Cook the mushrooms down until almost dry, then add some teriyaki to taste.

### EXTRA DETAIL
We keep cooked mushrooms handy. We cook them in large quantities and freeze them. They are good by themselves or added to other recipes. We start with 2 to 3 pounds and cook them down slowly. To get them started, add a little water or wine. They take a long time to cook down, so they are a good thing to make when having a cooking frenzy.

Cooked mushrooms weigh half as much as raw mushrooms. So, if a recipe calls for 1 pound of mushrooms, half a pound of cooked mushrooms will work. I use a scale when I package my mushrooms to freeze. I freeze in half-pound quantities and quarter-pound quantities. I use mugs for the half pounds and baggies for the quarter pounds.

before cooking ↑

after cooking ↑

# MUSHROOM GRAVY

## INGREDIENTS
1 diced onion
1 package mushrooms, diced small (14 ounces or whatever your store sells them in)
2 tablespoons tamari
2 tablespoons nutritional yeast
1 tablespoon Worcestershire
3 cups vegetable broth or water
1 tablespoon flour, mixed with a little water
2 tablespoons miso

## THE ESSENTIALS
Sauté the onions and mushrooms down about half way, then add everything but the flour. Bring to boil and add the premixed flour while whisking. Add only the amount of flour you need to get the thickness you desire.

## EXTRA DETAIL
Serve on bread, rice, white potatoes, etcetera.

This makes a big batch. I freeze most of it in mugs.

Premix the flour with a little water. Add just enough water to get a liquid instead of a paste. Stir rapidly when adding the premixed flour to the gravy.

# POTATO SALAD

## INGREDIENTS

2 to 2 ½ pounds red potatoes, cooked and sliced
½ onion diced and/or 2 stalks of celery, diced
¼ cup white vinegar
2 tablespoons water
2 tablespoons maple syrup
2 tablespoon whole-wheat flour
2 tablespoons nutritional yeast
pepper

## THE ESSENTIALS

Put the flour and nutritional yeast in a mixing bowl and stir while adding the wet ingredients. Then start adding potatoes until you are happy with the potato-to-goo ratio.

## EXTRA DETAIL

Scrub and remove bad spots. Poke the potatoes with a fork and nuke until the fork easily sticks into them. Any potato will do but the red potatoes do a little less falling apart (although the falling apart and crumbling doesn't hurt anything).

I usually slice the potatoes right out of the nuker. But it would be smarter to let them cool down first. I like this recipe hot or cold.

I like to cut the slices in half to make the pieces a little smaller.

RECIPES

SIDE DISHES

# SWEET POTATOES

### INGREDIENTS
sweet potatoes

### THE ESSENTIALS
Scrub, cut off bad spots, poke with a fork, and bake at 400 degrees until they are fork-soft, about 60 to 70 minutes.

### EXTRA DETAIL
I make an aluminum-foil pan to put them on. I suppose you could put them on a baking sheet, but I think some of the goo would be hard to clean off. It is a bit wasteful, but there's no pan to clean up.

After the potatoes cool, I cover them in the refrigerator and we saw off a chunk for dinner each night.

I do not recommend nuking sweet potatoes. They taste much better when they are baked. For white potatoes, I can't tell any difference.

### I YAM. I YAM WHAT I YAM.

I yam full of fiber and micronutrients. I can be eaten raw. 1 medium = about 100 calories. Loaded with vitamins A, magnesium, vitamin C, and many other vitamins.

# TWO-MINUTE VEGGIE FRENZY

### INGREDIENTS
veggies of your choice... We usually use green beans, spinach, Brussels sprouts, asparagus, broccoli, and corn on the cob.

### THE ESSENTIALS
We put about an inch of water in a big frying pan and boil each veggie for 2 minutes, covered, Brussels sprouts for 4 to 6 minutes.

### EXTRA DETAIL
We have a little battery-operated timer set to 2 minutes. When you stop and restart it, it restarts at 2 minutes again — very handy. When we're done, we boil down the remaining water and freeze it for veggie broth. You could also boil up your chopped-up and cleaned veggie trimmings at this time, or sometimes we just throw them in the freezer to boil later for broth. By saving the stock, you're saving the nutrients for use in another recipe. Steaming veggies takes longer, but preserves more nutrients.

asparagus ↓

maybe some corn, too ↓

veggies ↑

fancier veggies ↑

RECIPES

SIDE DISHES

# WHITE POTATOES

## INGREDIENTS
white potatoes, or yellow or red

## THE ESSENTIALS
Scrub to clean. Cut off any bad spots. Poke with a fork a few times. Nuke for about 2 to 4 minutes, depending on the potato and your microwave, until a fork sticks in easily.

## EXTRA DETAIL
Idea 1: Quarter lengthwise and eat like large French fries. Dip into ketchup or mustard.

Idea 2: Put on plate and squish with a fork. Top with Parmesan cheese (WFPB, page 99), non-dairy milk, pepper, gravy, etc. Use your imagination and look in the fridge.

Idea 3: Make a bunch and refrigerate the extras. They work well for ideas 1 and 2 cold. They are also good to eat plain as a filling snack.

# MISO SOUP

## INGREDIENTS
1 can Cannellini beans, 15-ounces, drained
1 carrot, diced
1 celery stalk, diced
1 ½ cups water
2 tablespoons white miso

## THE ESSENTIALS
Put everything but the miso in a pan and bring to a boil. Simmer for 15 to 20 minutes. Take off of the stove, and then add the miso. Stir well.

## EXTRA DETAIL
I use Hikari miso that I get online. I mention the specific miso I use because there seem to be a lot of different ones out there, and I have had some that I don't care for.

## NOTE
Why do you add the miso later? The more you heat miso the more you damage some of its nutrients. I add it after cooking with the hope that I am preserving more nutrients.

# MISO HEAT & EAT SOUP

## INGREDIENTS
1 can white beans, drained and rinsed, 15 ounces
1 can peas, use empty bean can to measure 15 ounces
1 can veggie broth or water, use bean can to measure 15 ounces
3 tablespoons white miso
1 tablespoon flour, if you want

## THE ESSENTIALS
Put the beans in a pot. Use the bean can to measure the peas, veggie broth, or water. Boil. Take off stove. Add miso. Stir. Eat.

## EXTRA DETAIL
If you would like the soup to have a little body, mix a tablespoon of flour with the water to make a thick paste. Stir this into the soup and bring to a boil. Stir for a while, the miso takes a bit of time to dissolve.

Kib's comment, "It doesn't look very appetizing, but it tastes okay." High praise.

See my notes about miso on the facing page. I prefer Hikari, and get it online. I also add miso later to try to preserve more nutrients.

# SPLIT PEA WITH SWEET POTATO SOUP

## INGREDIENTS
1 large onion, diced
2 carrots, diced
2 celery stalks, diced
2 big globs of miso (about 3 or 4 tablespoons)
1 bay leaf
2 teaspoons rosemary
2 teaspoons thyme
1 teaspoon smoked paprika
1 large sweet potato, diced (I like small cubes about ½ to ¼ inch)
2 cups split peas (a one-pound bag of dried peas)
8 cups veggie broth or water
pepper and/or hot sauce to taste

## THE ESSENTIALS
I suppose you could sauté the onions first, but I don't. I put all of the ingredients in a pot and turn on the heat. Bring to a boil and simmer it for 90 minutes or so, until you're happy with how the split peas are cooked.

## EXTRA DETAIL
This ends up being very thick, which I like. After it is cooked, add more water or veggie broth if you want it thinner. I put it in the refrigerator to cool, and then freeze it in coffee mugs.

RECIPES

SOUPS

# TOMATO PARSLEY SOUP

## INGREDIENTS
2 garlic cloves, diced
1 onion
1 small bunch parsley, cut up
    (a loosely-packed cup)
¼ cup cashews
1 cup water
1 can diced tomatoes, 28 ounces
2 tablespoons nutritional yeast
2 tablespoons miso
black pepper
hot sauce

## THE ESSENTIALS
Sauté onion and garlic in water or wine.

Add the tomatoes and parsley and boil for a few minutes.

Put the nuts, water, and nutritional yeast in a blender on high for 45 seconds.

Combine both mixtures in the blender on low speed for few seconds.

Bring to a second boil. Add miso, hot sauce, and pepper.

The soup is thick and will bubble out of the pan if heated too rapidly. So heat slowly, stir often, and keep it covered.

## EXTRA DETAIL
This was going to be tomato-basil soup, but I could rarely find fresh basil in the grocery store, so I tried parsley. I think it's good. Of course, you could substitute basil for parsley.

You could substitute any non-dairy milk for the cashews and water.

# RANCH DRESSING

### INGREDIENTS

½ cup raw, unsalted cashews
2 tablespoons raisins
½ teaspoon onion powder
1 teaspoon dill weed, dried
2 tablespoons white wine vinegar
1 teaspoon Bragg liquid aminos
½ cup water
1 teaspoon ground flaxseed

### THE ESSENTIALS

Add all to a blender and blend until smooth.

### EXTRA DETAIL

This is a good veggie dip. If you don't add the ground flaxseed it will be thinner and more suitable for salad dressing.

I served this dressing with raw veggies to a bunch of diehard carnivores, and they all liked it.

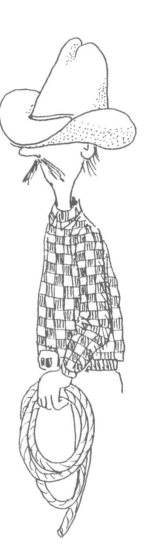

# TRI DRESSING

## INGREDIENTS
1 cup water
¼ cup balsamic vinegar
¼ cup lemon juice
¼ cup miso
¼ cup maple syrup
3 tablespoons ground flaxseed
¼ cup nutritional yeast
3 tablespoons yellow
        or Dijon mustard
½ teaspoon cayenne pepper
2 teaspoons turmeric
2 teaspoons black pepper

## THE ESSENTIALS
Add the wet ingredients to the blender. With the blender going, slowly add the dry ingredients. Then blend on high speed for a few seconds.

## EXTRA DETAIL
I make it in double batches and put most of it in a quart mason jar and the rest in a squeeze bottle.

This is my go-to dressing. You need a go-to dressing that you like. If this is not it, play around and search until you come up with an oil-free, salt-free dressing you like.

The name for this came from three dressing recipes I was using. I started mixing the three and playing around until I came up with this dressing, which became my favorite.

# SNACKS, DESSERTS & MORE

# ANTS ON A LOG

**INGREDIENTS**
raisins
peanut butter
celery

**THE ESSENTIALS**
Put peanut butter on celery.
Cover with raisins.

# CHOCOLATE MUFFINS

## INGREDIENTS
1 cup pitted Medjool dates, tightly packed
1 ¼ cups water
1 cup sprouted wheat flour or 1 heaping cup old-fashioned rolled oats
2 tablespoons ground flaxseeds
1 tablespoon baking powder
⅓ cup cacao powder

## THE ESSENTIALS
Blend the water, flour (or old-fashioned rolled oats), and dates in a food processor until smooth. Add the rest of the ingredients and blend until well mixed. Put into high-quality baking cups in a muffin pan and bake at 350 for 25 minutes. Remove from papers and put on a cooling rack as soon as possible.

## EXTRA DETAIL
I use PaperChef parchment large baking cups. Cheap muffin cups can stick to the muffins.

This makes 12 muffins.

RECIPES

SNACKS

# GRANOLA BARS, BANANA

## INGREDIENTS
1 cup Medjool dates, pitted
   *tightly packed (about 10 dates)*
2 ripe bananas
½ cup water
1 teaspoon vanilla
2 cups old-fashioned rolled oats
½ cup pumpkin seeds
½ cup almonds, sliced
½ cup walnuts or pecans
2 tablespoons chia seeds

## THE ESSENTIALS
Mix the bananas, dates, vanilla, and water in a food processor until smooth.
Put all of the other ingredients in a large bowl.

Mix the two together with a big spoon. Spread evenly on a cookie sheet lined
with parchment paper.

Bake at 350 degrees for 20 minutes. Flip it over. I use a spatula and cut it into 6
or so large chunks, then flip each chunk.

Bake another 20 minutes and check it. I usually bake it a little longer to brown it
up some.

## EXTRA DETAIL
Cool it on a cooling rack, put it in a plastic bag, and freeze.

Then just break off a chunk when you want a snack. You can eat it right out of
the freezer or thawed.

RECIPES

SNACKS

# MUFFINS, OAT-BRAN

## INGREDIENTS
3 cups oat bran
1 teaspoon baking powder
4 tablespoons maple syrup
2 tablespoons lemon juice
1 large apple, grated
6 bananas, the riper the better
¾ cup water
½ cup walnuts, chopped
¼ cup raisins

## THE ESSENTIALS
Put the baking powder and oat bran in a food processor and mix.
Use a dull blade if you have one. Add the rest of the ingredients, except for the
nuts and raisins, and mix. Then add the nuts and raisins, and barely mix.

Put into a muffin pan with high-quality muffin papers. I use Paperchef culinary
parchment large baking cups. (I have found other muffin cups stick to the
muffins.) Bake at 375 degrees for 40 minutes. Makes 24 muffins.

## EXTRA DETAIL
I have a food processor that has a dull and a sharp blade. For this recipe I
prefer the dull blade. If using a sharp blade, it may be better to mix the nuts
and raisins in with a spoon.

I remove the muffins as soon as I take them out of the oven and put them on a
cooling rack. Or, if you don't have a cooling rack, just set them upside-down on
a plate. If you leave them in the muffin tin, sometimes the bottoms get moist.

These freeze well, so make a bunch and freeze most
of them. To thaw, just leave out or nuke briefly.

I put them in the refrigerator to cool, before storing
in an airtight container or baggies, otherwise
condensation will form in the container.

# FUDGE (low-temperature cook)

## INGREDIENTS

1 can black beans, drained and rinsed, or 1½ cups cooked black beans
1 cup pitted Medjool dates, tightly packed
2 tablespoons peanut butter
1 teaspoon vanilla
½ cup cacao powder
1 tablespoon chia seeds
Enough water to get the food processor to process (about 4 tablespoons)

## THE ESSENTIALS

Combine everything except the cacao powder in a food processor. Process until smooth. Add the cacao and blend again. Put into very lightly greased 8-inch x 8-inch pan and bake at 200 degrees for 2 to 3 hours. Cool and cut into squares.

## EXTRA DETAIL

You are not really baking, you are drying. Keeping it at a maximum of 200 degrees is important because above that temperature it will start to deteriorate some of the healthful benefits of the cacao.

I put a tiny bit of oil in the pan and wipe it around with a paper towel. Then I get a clean paper towel and wipe it down again.

Any size pan will do. The thinner you make it, the less drying time it will need.

# FUDGE, CHOCOLATE MINT

### INGREDIENTS
8 Medjool dates, pitted
⅓ cup nut butter, I use almond or peanut
⅓ cup cacao powder
⅛ teaspoon peppermint extract
½ teaspoon vanilla extract

### THE ESSENTIALS
Add all ingredients to food processor and mix until it sticks together.
Put it in a pile on parchment paper.
Put parchment paper on top and press it down and flatten it out.
Cut into nice little squares.
The part that is left over after cutting nice squares can be rolled into balls or
eaten as is.

### EXTRA DETAIL
I also make this in a double batch. When I do that, I put it in an 8-inch x 8-inch
pan and press it down with a large spoon to compact it.

# PUDDING, CHOCOLATE

## INGREDIENTS
½ cup raw cashews
1 cup water
½ pound silken tofu
3 Medjool dates, pitted
2 tablespoons maple syrup
1 teaspoon vanilla
2 tablespoons cacao
1 tablespoon cornstarch or flour

## THE ESSENTIALS
Put all of the ingredients into a high-speed blender on high for 45 seconds. Move to a pan and bring to a boil, whisking constantly. Pour into 4 bowls.

## EXTRA DETAIL
This is just my cream sauce recipe with a few items added to make it into pudding.

Because of the cashews and tofu, this is a protein-packed dessert with very little sweetener. If you wanted to eliminate the maple syrup, you could add more dates and no maple syrup.

# PUDDING, CHIA

### INGREDIENTS
1 cup non-dairy milk
¼ cup chia seeds
2 teaspoons maple syrup
½ teaspoon vanilla

### THE ESSENTIALS
Mix together with a spoon and refrigerate for at least 1 hour.

### EXTRA DETAIL
This is super easy to make, tastes very good, and is good for you.

Dream up your own ideas. Just start with a ratio of 4 parts non-dairy milk to 1 part chia seeds, and the sweetener of your choice.

Stop there or add fruit, berries, cinnamon, coconut flakes, etcetera.

# PUDDING, VANILLA

## INGREDIENTS
½ cup raw cashews
1 cup water
½ pound silken tofu
3 Medjool dates, pitted
1 teaspoon vanilla
1 tablespoon cornstarch or flour

## THE ESSENTIALS
Put all of the ingredients into a high-speed blender on high for 45 seconds. Move to a pan and bring to a boil, whisking constantly. Pour into four bowls.

## EXTRA DETAIL
This is just my cream sauce recipe with a few items added to make pudding.

Because of the cashews and tofu, this is a protein-packed dessert with very little sweetener. This is not a very sweet pudding, but quite good. If you want it sweeter, add more dates or some maple syrup.

# PIE, PUMPKIN

### INGREDIENTS

1 can pumpkin puree, 15 ounces
10 ounces silken tofu
1 teaspoon pumpkin pie spice
1 cup Medjool dates, pitted, tightly packed

### THE ESSENTIALS

Blend in a food processor until smooth. Bake at 350 degrees for 60 minutes.

### EXTRA DETAIL

I use a small (8 ½-inch) pie pan.

This does not come out in pretty slices like a pie with a crust. It tastes good, but will look a little funky when served.

RECIPES

DESSERTS

# SWEET POTATO CACAO SPREAD

## INGREDIENTS
1 sweet potato
6 tablespoons date sugar
6 tablespoons cacao powder
water

## THE ESSENTIALS
Cook the potato at 425 degrees for 50 to 60 minutes, until soft.

Remove the skin and mix in all of the ingredients by hand.

Add enough water to get whatever consistency you want.

Peanut butter is also a good addition.

Serve on any whole-grain, salt-free cracker.

# BREAD

## SPROUTED WHEAT BREAD, USING A BREAD MACHINE

### INGREDIENTS
12 ounces water (1½ cups)
1½ teaspoons salt
¼ cup maple syrup
20 ounces sprouted wheat flour (4 cups)
1 packet Red Star dry active yeast
½ cup pumpkin seeds, if you want

### THE ESSENTIALS
Add the wet ingredients first, then the dry ones. I set my machine to medium crust and 2½-pound loaf. Cool 6 hours before slicing.

### EXTRA DETAIL
I have not found a sprouted bread in the store that I like. But I like this sprouted bread.

My machine has a place I can put the pumpkin seeds in, and the machine automatically adds them to the dough at the appropriate time. However, for that to work, I must remember to close a little door. When I forget to close the little door, the pumpkin seeds fall into the ingredients right at the start. I can't tell the difference, so I think it is okay to just add the pumpkin seeds at the beginning.

You can be very lax about measurements for most of my recipes, but not this one. If you have a scale, I recommend using it. This is the only recipe of mine that uses salt. I tried eliminating it and reducing it, but got lousy results. I believe this bread recipe needs the salt and maple syrup for chemical reactions with the yeast.

I apologize for suggesting a specific brand of yeast, but this is what has been working for me. I assume other yeasts would work fine, but am not sure. One packet of Red Star active dry yeast = 2½ teaspoons.

RECIPES

MISC

Let the bread cool for several hours or overnight on a cooling rack, then slice it, bag it, and freeze it. I bag it loosely and place it in the freezer carefully, so the slices aren't jammed together. That way the slices don't sick to each other when frozen.

If you can't wait and you slice it before its totally cool that is fine, but the bread will be sticky and hard to cut.

I have tried bread knives and fancy wooden slicing racks to get perfectly sliced bread. None of that worked for me. Now I put it on a cutting board and cut it with and electric knife. I just eyeball it. The slices don't come out perfectly even, but they come out close enough for me.

I have had good luck using King Arthur sprouted wheat flour and One Degree organic sprouted whole-wheat flour.

This recipe may work for handmade bread. I have no idea. I'm all about convenience and I love my bread machine for that.

### TROUBLESHOOTING

When I started making bread, I couldn't get it to rise very far. I found a bread troubleshooting guide and got the following information that helped me zero in on my ingredients.

Loaf rises too high:
        decrease liquid by a tablespoon or two,
        increase salt by ¼ teaspoon,
        decrease sweetener,
        decrease yeast.

Loaf doesn't rise high enough:
        inverse of above.

loaf ↓

sliced ↓

# CASHEW MILK

### INGREDIENTS
4 cups water
1 cup raw cashews
3 Medjool dates, pitted

### THE ESSENTIALS
Blend in high-speed blender for 45 seconds. Enjoy.

### EXTRA DETAIL
Since this is not filtered like other nut milks, it is very high in fat. But oh boy, is it good!

Any cashew milk you save should be shaken or stirred. Or should I say shaken, not stirred?

If you are using a low-speed blender, soak the cashews for several hours first.

cashew
→

# CHOCOLATE MILK

### INGREDIENTS
6 Medjool dates, pitted
½ cup raw cashews
2 cups water
3 teaspoons cacao

### THE ESSENTIALS
Blend in high-speed blender for 45 seconds.

chocolate
→

RECIPES

MISC

# COFFEE WITH CACAO

### INGREDIENTS
coffee
water
cacao

### THE ESSENTIALS
Add a teaspoon of cacao to a cup of coffee. Stir.

### EXTRA DETAIL
Cacao is loaded with antioxidants, fiber, and nutrients, so to get some of its benefits, every day I add a teaspoon to my black coffee in the morning.

The first few times I thought it was awful, but now I prefer my coffee with a teaspoon of cacao.

I brew my coffee the day before, so it is cold in the morning. I nuke a mug of it to warm it up. But I don't want it too warm because high heat would kill a lot of the antioxidants in the cacao. If I have hot, just-brewed coffee, I put a small ice cube in it before adding the cacao. I just want to make sure the coffee is under 200 degrees F.

I agree, Dave — The coffee tastes better knowing what a GENIUS our grandson is.

# BLUEBERRY JELLY

### INGREDIENTS
2 cups frozen blueberries
2 tablespoons water
2 tablespoons maple syrup
3 tablespoons chia seeds
1 tablespoon lemon juice

### THE ESSENTIALS
Bring the water, berries, and maple syrup to a boil and simmer for 15 minutes.
Let it cool a little bit, then add the chia seeds and lemon.

### EXTRA DETAIL
I use frozen berries. Adjust the recipe to the size of the bag you have. This should
work with fresh berries as well.

RECIPES

MISC

# PARMESAN CHEESE (WFPB)

## IMITATION & PRETTY TASTY

### INGREDIENTS
½ cup almonds
½ cup walnuts
½ cup nutritional yeast
1 tablespoon Table Tasty (this recipe is worth the special ingredient)

### THE ESSENTIALS
Use a food processor. Put everything in and process at full speed for 30 to 60 seconds.

### EXTRA DETAIL
I use this on spaghetti and baked potatoes. I also put a spoonful of it on toast to eat with my spaghetti. It's a little messy, but good.

You can use whatever nuts you want, or happen to have around.

Table Tasty is expensive and if exposed to humidity turns into a solid block. If you use Table Tasty, this is a good recipe to use clumped-up Table Tasty in, because it gets blended.

# VEGGIE BROTH

### INGREDIENTS
vegetable remains
water

### THE ESSENTIALS
When having a veggie frenzy, rinse and dice up the cutoffs that would typically be thrown away. Put in a pan with 1 to 2 inches of water covering the vegetables, bring to a boil, cover, then simmer for 45 minutes.

### EXTRA DETAIL
I usually freeze the vegetable cutoffs until I need veggie broth for something. You can add herbs if you like.

Boiled veggies are not as vitamin and antioxidant packed as steamed. But the vitamins and antioxidants don't just disappear, they end up in the water. So, it is important to save your water after boiling vegetables. Even when I steam veggies the water gets discolored, so I save that water also. Boiled or steamed, the broth can be concentrated by boiling it down. I always keep a stock of broth in the freezer.

## GETTING THE MOST OUT OF GREENS

Nutritionfacts.org highlights some studies have shown that in order to best preserve the cancer-fighting agents in greens, either cut them and then wait 40 minutes before cooking, or add a small bit of mustard powder to them after they are cooked. See their video: https://nutritionfacts.org/video/second-strategy-to-cooking-broccoli/.

pumpkins, meatloaf

kale, blueberries

smoothies!

grrr...
i can't find any eggs.
i like eggs.

EASY-GOING PLANT-BASED

# INDEX
## OF RECIPES & INGREDIENTS

# INGREDIENTS INDEX

# RECIPES INDEX

INDEX

# ICONS INDEX

##  Quick

Anytime breakfast bowl 37
Smoothie, kale, fruit, spices 38
Beginner breakfast bowl 42
Smoothie, fruit 43
Black beans and rice 46
Hot dogs (carrot) 53
Rice and veggies 57
Spaghetti 60
Tacos 61
Kale 67
Potato salad 72
Two-minute veggie frenzy 74
White potatoes 75
Miso heat and eat soup 77
Ranch dressing 80
Tri dressing 81
Ants on a log 83
Fudge, chocolate mint 88
Pudding, chocolate 89
Pudding, vanilla 91
Cashew milk 96
Chocolate milk 96
Coffee with cacao 97
Parmesan cheese 99

##  Carnivore guests

Barbecue pulled pork 45
Black beans and rice 46
Burgers 47
Cashew rice 48
Chili 49
Hot dogs (carrot) 53
Lentil stew or sloppy Joe 54
Mushroom stroganoff or gravy 56
Meatloaf 58
Ground meat substitute 59
Spaghetti 60
Baked beans 63
Mushrooms 70
Mushroom gravy 71
Potato salad 72
Sweet potatoes 73
Split pea sweet potato soup 78
Tomato parsley soup 79
Ranch dressing 80

##  Simple (few ingredients)

Smoothie, kale, fruit, spices 38
Barbecue pulled pork 45
Black beans and rice 46
Chili 49
Cream sauce 50
Hot dogs (carrot) 53
Rice and veggies 57
Spaghetti 60
Tacos 61
Beets 64
Creamed turnips 65
French fries (not fried) 66
Kale 67
Mashed potatoes 68
Mashed potato slop 69
Mushrooms 70
Potato salad 72
Sweet potatoes 73
Two-minute veggie frenzy 74
White potatoes 75
Miso soup 76
Miso heat and eat soup 77
Ants on a log 83
Pudding, chia 90
Pumpkin pie 92
Sweet potato cacao spread 93
Cashew milk 96
Chocolate milk 96
Coffee with cacao 97
Blueberry jelly 98
Parmesan cheese 99
Veggie broth 100

##  Sweet

Breakfast bowls 37, 42
Smoothie, kale, fruit, spices 38
Smoothie, fruit 43
Chocolate muffins 84
Granola bars, banana 85
Oat-bran muffins 86
Fudges 87, 88
Pudding, chocolate 89
Pudding, chia 90
Pudding, vanilla 91
Pumpkin pie 92
Sweet potato cacao spread 93
Cashew milk 96
Chocolate milk 96
Blueberry jelly 98

## ❄ Freezer leftovers

Barbecue pulled pork 45
Black beans and rice 46
Burgers 47
Cashew rice 48
Cream sauce 50
Creamed veggies, rice, pasta 52
Lentil stew or sloppy Joe 54
Rice and veggies 57
Meatloaf 58
Ground meat substitute 59
Baked beans 63
Kale 67
Mushrooms 70
Mushroom gravy 71
Split pea sweet potato soup 78
Granola bars, banana 85
Bread 94

## Snacks

Anytime breakfast bowl 37
Smoothie, kale, fruit, spices 38
Beginner breakfast bowl 42
Smoothie, fruit 43
Hot dogs (carrot) 53
Rice and veggies 57
Beets 64
French fries (not fried) 66
Mushrooms 70
Potato salad 72
White potatoes 75
Ranch dressing 80
Ants on a log 83
Chocolate muffins 84
Granola bars, banana 85
Oat-bran muffins 86
Fudge, low-temp bake 87
Fudge, chocolate mint 88
Pudding, chocolate 89
Pudding, chia 90
Pudding, vanilla 91
Sweet potato cacao spread 93
Bread 94
Cashew milk 96
Chocolate milk 96
Blueberry jelly 98

INDEX